VICE D'HIVE

& LOGE

Y

Pélerin. Charlot pasteu   819

ESCALIER D

CUISINES GAUCHE

THE NATURAL HOME.

THE
NATURAL
HOME.

HANS BLOMQUIST
PHOTOGRAPHY BY DEBI TRELOAR

RYLAND
PETERS
& SMALL
LONDON NEW YORK

Senior designer Megan Smith
Commissioning editor
Annabel Morgan
Location research Jess Walton
Production Gordana Simakovic
Art director Leslie Harrington

First published in 2012 by
Ryland Peters & Small
20–21 Jockey's Fields
London WC1R 4BW
and
519 Broadway, 5th Floor
New York, NY 10012
www.rylandpeters.com
10 9 8 7 6 5 4 3 2 1

Text © Hans Blomquist 2012
Design and photographs
© Ryland Peters & Small 2012

ISBN: 978-1-84975-213-8

A CIP record for this book is
available from the British Library.

Library of Congress CIP data
has been applied for.

Printed and bound in China

contents.

introduction.

IT'S HARD TO PUT A LABEL ON YOUR OWN STYLE, but when I try to define my look I keep coming back to the word 'natural'. I love the innate imperfection of natural materials, I love nature itself and I love homes that seem to have evolved and grown naturally to reflect the personalities of their inhabitants. Another great inspiration is my passion for vintage objects, which started at a very early age – I can remember rummaging in my grandmother's attic as a small child, looking for discarded treasures. As the years have passed, little has changed and I still have a weakness for all things antique or vintage. Today, such items are a source of inspiration not only for my own home, but also in my work as an art director and stylist. My style has developed over the years, but the ingredients remain the same: muted colours, atmospheric still lifes composed of vintage pieces, the textures of the natural world, tactile natural fabrics, and, of course, plants and foliage, which bring vivid colour to the moody colour schemes I love best. As well as focusing on these elements of my style, in this book I offer a glimpse of real-life homes that I find particularly inspiring – homes that share my own design aesthetic and have a uniquely 'natural' charm of their own.

THE
NATURAL
ELEMENTS.

AMAZING BULB.
Colchicum bulbs are amazing. They can be 'forced' into bloom just by placing the bare bulb on a sunny windowsill (far left).

JUST SIMPLE.
A small rattan basket is home to a succulent plant (left).

EASY TO GROW.
In winter, berried branches add vivid colour to the landscape. I love to bring them inside, where they dry out and remain beautiful (opposite).

plants and foliage.

FOR ME, PLANTS AND FOLIAGE ARE AN ESSENTIAL ELEMENT OF ANY HOME: they bring an interior to life. Even better, they absorb carbon dioxide and are very effective at purifying the air, removing pollutants and toxins such as formaldehyde. I leave my plants to grow freely – I don't like anything too manicured or too neat, preferring a random, jungly effect. Some of my favourites are scented geraniums for their wonderful perfume, *Sparmannia africana* for its large, light green leaves and *Muehlenbeckia complexa*, which grows with great vigour and has a dense tangle of dark stems. In the natural home, foliage or flowers should be as close to nature as possible: think of a long branch studded with blossom in spring, an armful of flowering grasses in summer, and bare, leafless twigs in autumn. A few simple stems or a loose bunch create the best effects. Lastly, gorgeous as they may be, hothouse blooms from the florist have no place in the natural home!

ARCHITECTURAL FORMS.
Dried cow parsley, also known as Queen Anne's Lace, has an intriguing silhouette. The woody stems harmonize with the faded gilt picture frames on the wall (this page).

TALL GRASS.
The drooping shape of these tall grasses echoes the form of the catkins on the botanical poster behind. The grasses are arranged in clear glass for maximum simplicity (opposite).

ON DISPLAY.

Humble pot plants make the perfect basis for creative arrangements, especially if you follow some tried and tested guidelines. First, use plenty of simple terracotta pots (above left, above and below right). Like good wine, they get better with age, developing a beautiful, tactile patina. Second, since almost anything can be used as a container, play around with what you have at home – you'll know when something looks right. Here, I've used an old galvanized-metal bucket (above right) and an antique fruit crate (below left). Finally, placing a plant on a pedestal, chair or small table gives far greater impact to the display (above and below centre).

A PALETTE OF GREENS.

Expensive exotics are not my style – I have a passion for pot plants, wildflowers and bulbs, all of which are cheap and easy to find. Even the most insignificant plants can bring a container to life (above centre). Many plants, such as sparmannia and geraniums (above left and below centre), are easy to propagate from cuttings – snip off a stem with two or three leaves on it, then stand it in water. When the roots are about an inch long, the cutting can be planted in compost. Bulbs are also easy to grow, like these ornithogalum (below right). If you don't have green fingers, simply cut a few stems from the garden (below left and above right).

LEAFY DISPLAYS.
Gather all your plants
together in one spot and
make your own miniature
botanical garden (this
page and opposite).

CABINET OF CURIOSITIES.
Using old fruit crates to frame smaller items makes for an interesting display, suggesting a cabinet of curiosities (opposite). If the items are fragile, use a glass cloche as a vitrine. Try lining up larger pieces along the top of a cabinet (far left) or pile them high (left).

WORK OF ART.
This very tonal display of items that share natural, neutral colours gives the effect of an oil painting (overleaf).

display.

I THINK I HAVE ALWAYS BEEN A COLLECTOR OF THINGS – both items that I have inherited and also objects picked up on my travels and kept as mementoes of a particular time and place. In addition, I spend a lot of time visiting antique shops and flea markets looking for interesting objects for my work, and I often stumble across irresistible treasures that I can't resist buying for my own home. One of my favourite pastimes is creating still lifes and displays that showcase my collections. A display can be made out of anything you like, whether it be a collection of items that share a common theme (like animals or fans or African carvings) or random things you have amassed over the years. My own personal treasures are all nearly all vintage, mainly because I love anything old and timeworn. There are no rules when it comes to creating displays or still lifes – just make sure they consist of things that you love and that are meaningful to you.

TONE ON TONE.
Both these atmospheric
displays rely on grouping
together items that share
colour and texture to create
a subtle, painterly effect
(previous spread).

GLASS CONTAINERS.
Glass vases and jars are a
great way to display smaller
items such as shells, dried
flowers and spools of thread
(this page).

BACKGROUND EFFECTS.
Old newspapers and
letters create an interesting
backdrop for a selection of
random objects (opposite).

there are no rules. WHEN IT COMES TO SUCCESSFUL DISPLAYS, THERE ARE NO RIGHTS
AND WRONGS. DON'T BE AFRAID TO EXPERIMENT AND TO TAKE A FEW DECORATING RISKS.

FRUTAL

1 Avenue Jeanne
ASNIÈRES (SEINE)

ESSENCES
NATURELLES
DE FRUITS

PARFUMS
SYNTHÉTIQUES

HUILES
ESSENTIELLES

VIOLET FONCÉ
INDÉLÉBILE
YANGTSE
J.M.PAILLARD·PARIS

THE JOY OF PAINT.
One of my favourite paint suppliers is Farrow & Ball, not only for the beautiful, subtle colours they have in their collection, but also because they strive to make eco-friendly paints. The colours shown here include Cord, Cornforth White, Charleston Grey, Mouse's Back and Cooking Apple Green (this spread).

colour.

COLOUR IS SUCH A PERSONAL THING. Some of us love bright, dazzling colours; others prefer muted shades; and some are drawn to the pure simplicity of black and white. Nature is an amazing inspiration and I always find myself returning to a subdued palette made up of colours found in the natural world – wet sand, earth, bark, dried flax, thunderclouds, fields of wheat, bare branches and vivid green spring growth. Using muted and sombre colours in your home will create a naturally tranquil and soothing atmosphere and will also provide an excellent backdrop for dashes of brighter colour or areas of pattern. I also like the effect of dark walls and the way they throw into relief lighter-coloured furnishings and objects, but if your home is lacking in natural light it may be that a paler, neutral scheme will make the most of the light that's available.

The colour scheme of the natural home ranges from off-white to deep charcoal grey. You can choose to work with just one or two colours throughout your home, or try using several colours to create a more layered, tonal effect (this page).

RCE 250 K⁰ˢ

PEELING PAINT.
To me, peeling paint is quite beautiful, revealing traces of an object's history and breathing life into the otherwise rather flat surfaces of painted furniture. I would never sand down or repaint an old piece of furniture – it destroys the alluring, hard-won patina of age (far left and below left).

NATURAL TEXTURES.
Look to nature for your colours, such as this earthy brown bird's nest or Felix the whippet and his soft, sleek mushroom coat (left and below right).

be inspired by the colours of nature. WET SAND, BARE EARTH, BARK, DRIED FLAX, THUNDERCLOUDS, FIELDS OF WHEAT, BARE BRANCHES AND SPRING LEAVES.

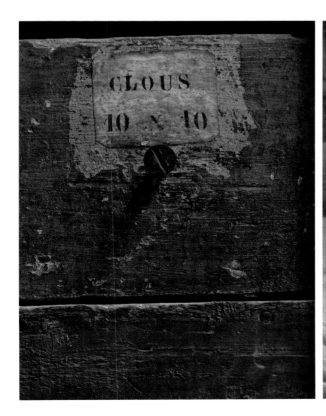

CHOOSING COLOURS.

It is not always easy to decide which colours to use in your home. Take inspiration from a few of your most cherished items, then try creating a mood board of the shades you like best. Live with it for a little while, to give you time to make the right decision (this page and opposite).

POINT OF CONTRAST.
A bare stone wall is the perfect textural backdrop for an assortment of old wooden objects. Spools of silky green thread provide a single dash of colour and contrasting texture (opposite).

BOOK LOVER.
I collect old books. Stacked up like this, their pages have a particularly intriguing texture (far left).

LOOSELY WOVEN.
Like all natural fibres, rattan ages really beautifully (left).

texture.

TEXTURE IS THE SECRET INGREDIENT AT THE HEART OF THE NATURAL HOME and it's the combination of different textures that adds depth, interest and richness to an interior. Think of scuffed and scarred wood, peeling paint, rusting metal, frayed fabric, bare stone or objects that have been worn and marked by the passage of time. I like to play around and layer texture upon texture in my home – the roughness of raw stone walls and unpainted wood alongside the softness of worn linen and the dull sheen of antique glass or murky, tarnished mirrors. To me, there is nothing more beautiful than an old piece of furniture or other seasoned object whose texture has been left untouched, and I think it is a shame when people buy antiques or vintage pieces and set about eradicating all traces of age. In the natural home, it's best to keep things simple and allow textures to speak for themselves.

NATURAL TEXTURES.

A chunky throw gives texture to any sofa or chair (above left). This is one of my favourite chairs, found in an antiques shop in Sweden; you can tell that it has seen hard use, both as a chair and a work bench (above centre). This yarn has been spun from vintage fabrics, creating an intriguing texture (above right). Old wooden boards add interest to a kitchen (below left). Slubby antique linen sheets have a unique feel (below centre). I love these wooden drawers with their old labels for the sense of history they convey (below right). Many people would throw away this tattered chaise longue, but to me it's worth keeping for its texture and colour (opposite).

SMOOTH STONE.
The visual appeal of this
old floor derives from the
way the stones have been
worn smooth by years
of use. (this page).

WORN WOOD.
Antique wooden doors
make an unusual headboard
for a bed (opposite).

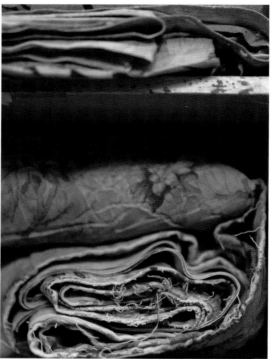

WOVEN TREASURES.
I have collected old French linen for years. It's beautiful, strong and long-lasting, perfect for loose covers or cushions. Simple graphic patterns, faded florals and botanical prints also work very well in the natural home (this spread).

SHOW OFF.
This dummy is dressed in the fragile lining of a vintage jacket, while the chairs opposite have been partly covered with faded printed cotton and old linen sacks (overleaf).

fabrics.

I LOVE FABRICS, ESPECIALLY VINTAGE FABRICS THAT HAVE BEEN WASHED and worn repeatedly over the years – their crumpled texture and faded hues are strangely appealing to me. French linen sheets are among the fabrics that I find most appealing – they are both practical and good-looking, and I have a hard time resisting them when I visit one of the many flea markets here in France. Textiles bring softness and warmth to any interior and I use them in every room – as loose covers on chairs and sofas, in the form of cushions, tablecloths and napkins, as cosy woollen blankets, or just folded and piled up on a chair as a still life. Fabrics should, of course, should be sourced from nature – no artificial materials in the natural home, please! When it comes to colour, I love neutral, undyed linens or cottons bleached by age and constant washing, but I am also drawn to darker shades such as charcoal grey, earthy brown and faded blue-black.

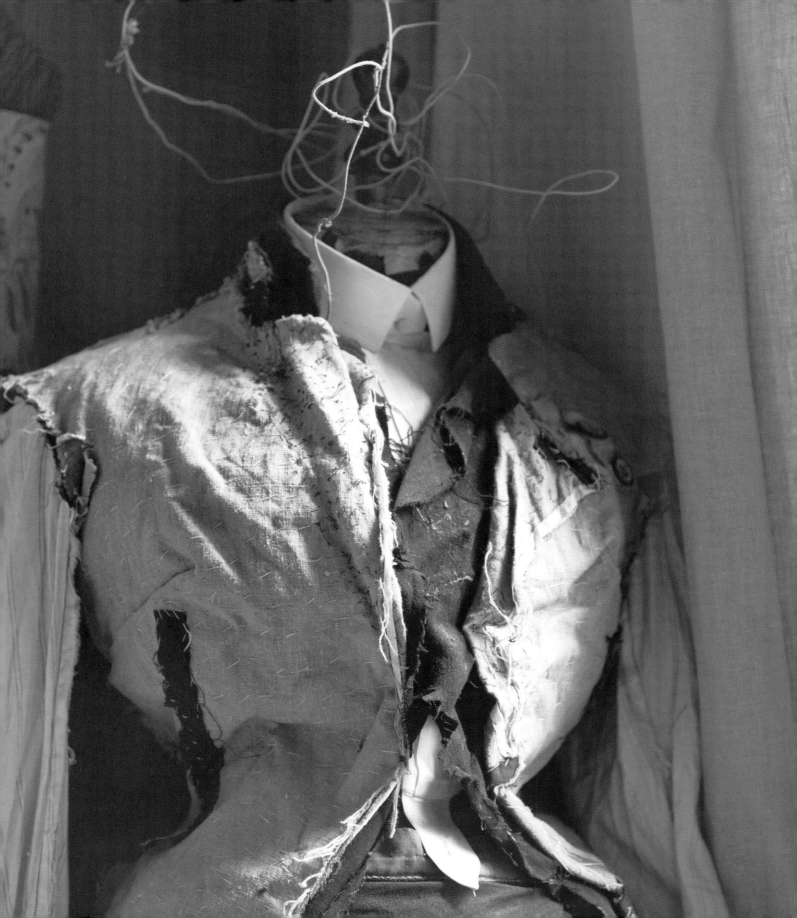

IN THE MIX.
Fabrics made from natural fibres are perfect for the natural home, but beyond that there are no rights or wrongs. Choose plain or printed; darker shades or pale neutrals. Faded florals look great mixed with more graphic prints. Patchwork is also a good addition (this spread).

GLORIOUS NEUTRALS.
Linen is a key material in the natural home. I love its range of hues, from flax to ecru to grey. I like to combine both fine and loose weaves with bold prints (overleaf).

vintage french linen sheets are one of my favourite things. AS WELL AS BED LINEN, THEY CAN BE USED AS UPHOLSTERY FABRIC OR TO MAKE CURTAINS, BLINDS AND TABLECLOTHS.

THE NATURAL HOMES.

PLANT STILL LIFE.
A fig branch in an old milk bottle is an inviting still life on a bedside table made from a battered tub once used for washing (far left).

SIMPLE RECYCLING.
A slender branch finds new life as a picture rail, while a battered armchair has been recovered in antique French linen (left and below).

ON THE SIDE.
An old trestle table, covered with a linen runner, is used to display antique wooden bowls and an arrangement of olive branches (opposite).

a rustic retreat.

CLOSE TO UZÈS IN THE GARD REGION OF FRANCE, ON THE EDGE OF A VILLAGE SURROUNDED BY VINEYARDS AND OLIVE GROVES, STANDS THIS FORMER FARMHOUSE, PARTS OF WHICH DATE BACK TO THE 18TH CENTURY. IT IS A SUBLIME EXAMPLE OF A NATURAL HOME.

The house is slightly tucked away from the road and there is nothing to disturb the peace and tranquillity. Entering through an old wooden door set in a stone wall, the visitor steps into a charming courtyard, presided over by a large and ancient fig tree, beneath which the owner, Josephine, an antiques dealer, and her guests seek shade on hot summer days.

Josephine's home is a cornucopia of French vintage and antique furniture combined with *objets trouvés*. Revering the craftsmanship of the past, she loves nothing more than to trawl through local flea markets in search of the next treasure.

keeping calm. NEUTRAL TONES OF CREAM AND WHITE, ALLIED WITH THE TEXTURES OF WOOD, LEATHER AND LINEN, CREATE A CALM FEEL IN THE MAIN LIVING AREA OF THIS OLD FARMHOUSE.

MIXING MATERIALS.
Even though modern in style, the cream leather
sofa seems perfectly at home in this traditional
rural setting. Its neutral tones complement the
original wooden floors and the antique furniture.
Still lifes of cherished objects, such as sculptural
wooden bowls, are displayed on functional trestle
table. The linen runner softens and lightens the
arrangement (this spread).

Despite Josephine's passion for antiques, nothing in this house is surplus to requirements, and the look she has created is pared down, relaxing and, above all, natural.

From the front door, a white wooden staircase with open treads leads up to the spacious living room, which during the daytime is flooded with natural light pouring in from its many windows. Untreated original wooden floorboards and white-painted walls form a plain backdrop to this bare-boned room. Neutral tones of cream and white, combined with wood, leather and linen, establish a soothing atmosphere. At perfect ease alongside the antique wooden tables and sideboards and armchairs upholstered in vintage French linen is a modern cream leather sofa. This single signature piece gives the room an interesting contemporary edge.

Elsewhere on the ground floor, an old, glass-paned door opens straight into the kitchen. Its low, vaulted stone ceiling, now painted white, reveals that this space was once the cellar, or *cave*, used to house farm animals. Sandwiched between antique wooden cabinets is a capacious range oven, which is more or less the only modern feature of the room. The wall opposite is covered with open shelves, also antique, and is home to an impressive collection of mismatched vintage china. The large traditional porcelain sink adds to the rustic feel of the space.

BARE ESSENTIALS.
There is not much to distract the attention in this unadorned office, where the floor, walls and ceiling are all painted white, to give the room a light and airy feel. Even the antique wooden desk has been treated to a coat of white paint, but the timeworn garden chair has been allowed to retain its original colour for contrast (above).

RUSTIC DINING.
Like the rest of the house, the dining room is simply furnished. An antique wooden table with white-painted dining chairs form the centrepiece (right).

PEELING PAINT.
A rustic cabinet that has lost most of its paint makes ideal storage for china and glasses (opposite).

At the opposite end of the kitchen is a small, informal dining area. Apart from a new, floor-to-ceiling, metal-framed window, installed to give a view over the garden, the room's original structure has been left untouched. The walls are a rough whitewashed stone, creating the ideal backdrop for a French bistro table and a set of simple folding chairs.

The adjacent dining room is sparsely furnished. A well-worn table takes centre stage, surrounded by antique, white-painted wooden chairs. Original terracotta floor tiles stay cool in summer, while the huge open fireplace keeps everyone snug in winter.

Along with Josephine's office, the master bedroom is upstairs. Containing only a modern wooden four-poster bed and a few chairs and stools, it is as calming a space as can be imagined.

RECLAIMED STORAGE.
Old cabinets and open shelves are used for storing kitchen essentials, while vintage cutlery is close to hand in ceramic pots. The low ceiling and walls in the cooking area are painted white to brighten up the space (this page).

NATURAL STONE.
The vaulted ceiling indicates that the kitchen was once a cellar. The original stonework in the dining area has deliberately been left untouched (opposite).

DISPLAYING COLLECTIONS.
Josephine has spent several years putting together this impressive collection of mismatching china, much of which has seen better days. The pieces are housed in an antique unit consisting of open shelves. In addition to making individual items easy to find, this type of storage is particularly well suited to items that form an attractive display in their own right. Traditional baskets add to the rustic appeal (this spread).

DRESSING UP.

In the dressing room, an industrial metal shelving unit on castors is used for storing everything from clothes to bed linen. Piled high and in plain view, the items present an enticing display of colours and textures. More fragile items of clothing are protected in the freestanding cupboard made of reclaimed wooden doors, while shoes are concealed in an oversized rattan basket (this spread).

soothing. THE MUTED COLOURS OF THE FABRICS VISIBLE ON THE OPEN SHELVES ENHANCE THE SOOTHING AMBIENCE OF THE DRESSING ROOM WITH ITS PALE BLUE SLATTED CEILING.

At the end of the bed, a large olive branch hangs from the ceiling like a chandelier. A metal-framed door leads onto the sun-flooded terrace – a lovely spot for an early morning coffee.

In keeping with the rest of the house, the guest accommodation is simply furnished with flea-market finds. Antique French linens cover the bed, while an upturned zinc dolly tub, once used for washing clothes, serves as a bedside table. Josephine has left one wall unplastered and unpainted to showcase the original stone structure of the building. The rest of the room, including the floor, is painted white.

Created out of the original *cave*, with its stone walls painted white, the ensuite bathroom has a fairytale feel. One tiny window allows soft light to filter through. There is just enough space for the antique bathtub to stand in the middle of the floor. Alongside, piled high with towels, a rattan peacock chair adds the finishing touch to this unusual space.

Josephine has collected all sorts of antique furniture and objects – some practical, others purely decorative – and combined them in an inspired but uncontrived way to create her take on the natural home. Recycling is a key element: old pieces are given a new lease of life through the way they are displayed or by the new roles they assume. Texture and colour play their part, too: a mix of wood, leather and linen and a limited palette of neutral colours, such as white, beige and cream, keep the look harmonious.

PEACEFUL SLEEP.
Neutral colours and natural materials shape the character of the master bedroom. At its centre is a plain, modern four-poster, covered in an antique linen sheet and flanked by wooden bedside stools (opposite).

LOUNGING AROUND.
With lovely rural views, the bedroom terrace is a haven of tranquillity (above right).

OLD AND NEW.
An antique slipper bath is paired with a modern swan-neck tap in the guest bathroom (right).

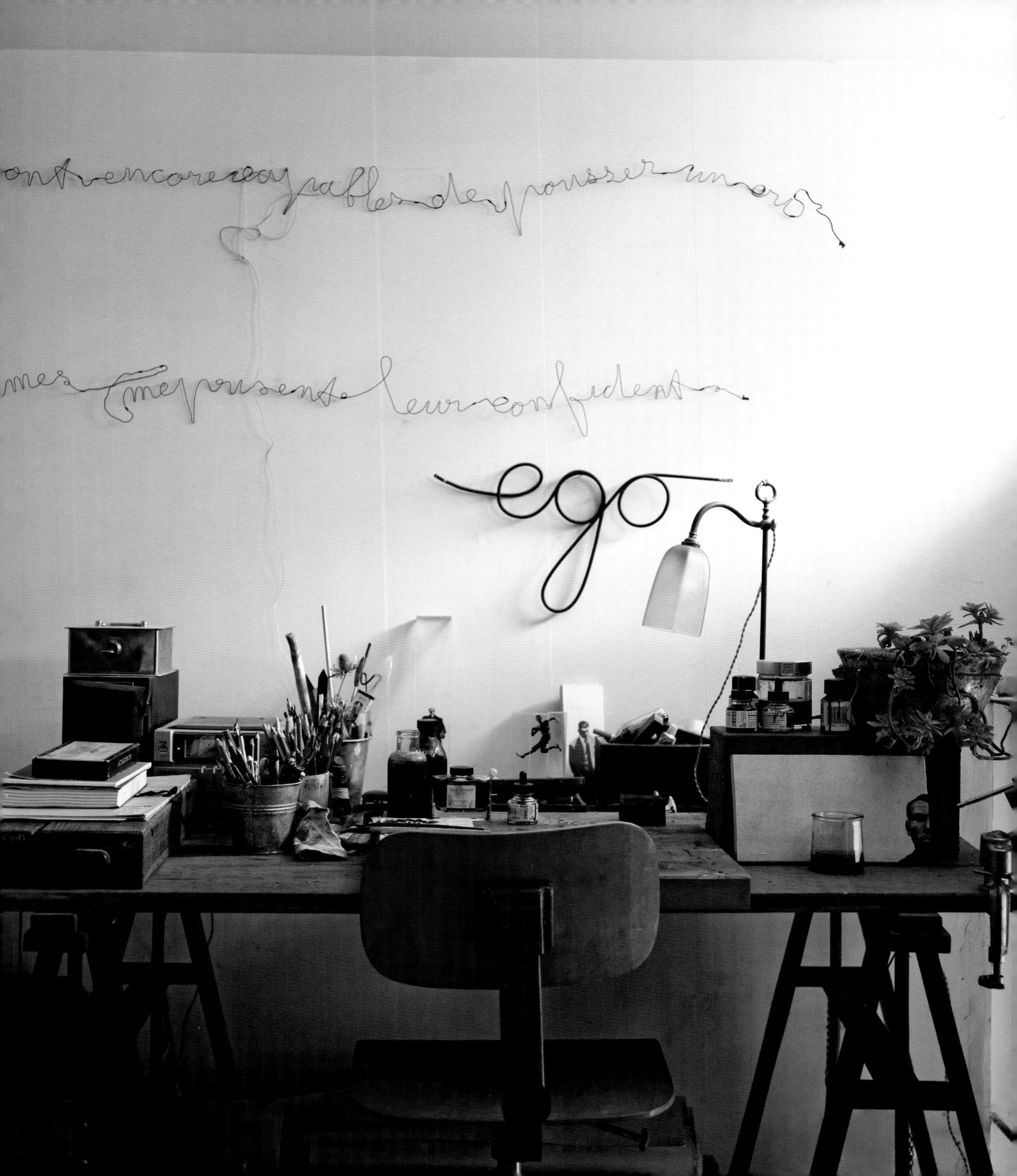
ego

ON DISPLAY.
Easy to make and easy
to take down and replace
is this office-wall display
of cards, sketches and
photographs hanging from
string and clothes pegs
(right). A collection of old
bottles and vases makes an
interesting still life in the
kitchen (far right).

CREATIVE THINKING.
Alfonso's office is sparsely
furnished with a trestle table
and a wooden chair. He
made the lines of poetry
on the wall from lengths of
thin metal wire (opposite).

the old button factory.

THIS INSPIRING HOME WAS CREATED FROM AN OLD BUTTON FACTORY SITUATED JUST
OUTSIDE PARIS. IT WAS REBUILT AND DESIGNED FROM SCRATCH BY THE OWNERS,
ALONSO, AN ARTIST, AND HIS WIFE, VIRGINIE, A TREND FORECASTER.

The factory had been divided up into five living spaces,
and when Alfonso and Virginie bought their house
it was no more than an empty shell. The couple set
about transforming it to meet their needs and suit their
particular lifestyle. They wanted to retain the industrial
spirit of the former factory, while creating a warm and
relaxed family home for themselves and their young
son. To achieve this, they used hard materials such as
concrete and metal, while including recycled wood
and muted colours to soften the edges. The result is
an undeniably contemporary yet comfortable home.

It was important to Alfonso and Virginie to retain
the sense of space that had characterized the original
building and, to this end, they decided to adopt a
largely open-plan layout. Windows at the front and
back windows extend all the way up to the roof,
flooding the space with natural light.

The main door opens directly into Alfonso's studio.
Paintings set up on easels and hanging on the walls,
a riot of colour and the distinctive smell of turpentine
combine to make a memorable welcome. Beyond the
studio is the kitchen/living area, with large windows

opening onto the small garden. Designed and built by the couple, the kitchen is an inviting space. Concrete and stainless steel feature throughout, but the uncompromising nature of these materials is offset by the recycled wood used for cupboard doors and drawers. The open shelf above the sink and work surface also contributes to the informal feel.

Butting up to the kitchen cupboards is a small antique cabinet, painted a soft green, which doubles as a display area for a still life featuring a favourite china vase and an eclectic mix of treasures unearthed at flea markets. Above the cabinet hangs a vintage botanical poster and beside this is a green wall cabinet, containing everyday glassware as well as a collection of antique medicine bottles. Both cabinets have been allowed to retain their original, slightly mismatching green colour to give even more personality to the room.

Although quite sparsely furnished, the kitchen/living area feels cosy, thanks to the clever juxtaposition of modern and traditional styles and hard and soft materials. The large metal dining table was specially designed and made by the couple to fit the space. A variety of 20th-century chairs surrounds it, while an array of cushions adorns the pale sofa. These have a softening effect on the lofty expanse of off-white walls and the polished-concrete floor.

The master bedroom is situated in the centre of the house on the ground floor. It has no outside windows so, in an inspired piece of design, the couple have inserted an internal window into one wall, allowing light to stream in from the tall windows in the kitchen/living area. At night, white linen curtains can be pulled across for privacy.

WARM WELCOME.
Softening elements give the contemporary living room a relaxed and welcoming feel. The large, neutral-coloured sofa is piled high with cushions in muted tones, while natural light gives a soft sheen to the polished-concrete floor. Alfonso painted the portrait hanging on the wall (right).

warmth and personality. EARTHY COLOURS AND TEXTURES PREVENT THIS MODERN AND INDUSTRIAL-STYLE KITCHEN FROM APPEARING COLD AND IMPERSONAL.

KITCHEN RECYCLING.

The concrete and brushed-steel fitted kitchen was designed by Alfonso and Virginie. In spite of these unforgiving materials, the space has a warm feel, achieved through the introduction of softer elements such as recycled wooden doors (this page).

DINING IN.

Vintage wooden chairs take the industrial edge off the dining area. The large sliding doors allow the room to be flooded with natural light (opposite).

ARTIST IN RESIDENCE.
The soft northern light streams into Alfonso's studio,
filled with canvasses, paints and brushes. His paintings
are propped up against the wall and set on easels,
while brushes of all shapes and sizes are kept in
various containers and glass pots, like flowers in a
vase. The industrial drawer unit has been fitted with
wheels so that it is easy to move around (this spread).

Like the rest of the house, the master bedroom has been decorated in muted tones. A large white bathtub in a concrete surround and a sink are just a few steps away from the low bed, adding a touch of decadence. The bedside table is made up of a collection of old drawer units and is used to display cherished flea-market finds. Above it hangs one of Alfonso's paintings.

Between the master bedroom and the artist's studio is their young son's room, designed with a child in mind. The bed is raised higher than normal and has easy-access storage underneath. Alfonso and Virginie put floorboards in this room, rather than concrete, so that the surface would be warmer and softer for their son to play on.

Stairs from the studio lead up to the mezzanine level, which is home to a guest room with a balcony on either side. The couple use these balconies as home offices and, thanks to the tall windows at each end of the house, they are filled with natural light.

Alfonso and Virginie have created a home that feels natural through and through, thanks to their clever design and use of materials. Old and new, wood and metal, concrete and glass are combined to create a family home with huge warmth and positive energy in this contemporary post-industrial space.

BOOK COLLECTION.
Clever use has been made of recesses and dead space for storing the couple's diverse collection of books. A custom-made bookcase has been squeezed into the tall and narrow recess by the stairs to the first floor, fitting it exactly and taking up no extra floor space (this page).

OFFICE WITH A VIEW.
Virginie's office is located on a mezzanine balcony overlooking the living area. The original windows on the ground floor are so tall that they fill this space with natural light. The vintage metal balustrade suits the industrial feel (this page).

SANCTUARY.

With the bathtub and the basin close by, the master bedroom is like an elegant hotel room but with much more character. Above the bedside table, made of old wooden drawers, is a painting by Alfonso. Fixed to the wall outside Leon's bedroom are cutout birds, a birdcage and wooden printer's type spelling his name (this page).

CHILD-LEVEL THINKING.

This bedroom has been very cleverly designed to suit the couple's young son, Leon. The bed has been raised higher than normal, and drawers have been incorporated underneath for storing toys. In contrast with the other rooms in the house, the floor is wooden, providing a warmer surface for Leon to play on (opposite).

MAKING A STATEMENT.
Flowering colchicum bulbs
with an antique vase
behind make an intriguing
composition, as does the
small stone statue presided
over by a spindly stemmed
succulent (far left and left).

SENSE OF SPACE.
The small kitchen has been
ingeniously built into an old
storage cupboard (below).

BUSINESS AND PLEASURE.
The muted colour scheme
in this shop/office space
creates a moody ambience.
Oliver designed the striking
shelf unit (opposite).

naturally moody.

IN THE MIDDLE OF COPENHAGEN, WITH ITS BUSTLE OF
CARS AND BIKES, LIVES OLIVER GUSTAV, AN INTERIOR
DESIGNER/ARCHITECT AND PART-TIME SHOPKEEPER.
ONCE YOU CLOSE THE STREET DOORS BEHIND YOU
AND ENTER THE COURTYARD BELOW HIS APARTMENT,
THE NOISE FADES AND IT'S HARD TO BELIEVE THAT YOU
ARE IN THE CENTRE OF A CROWDED MODERN CITY.

Oliver lives on the first floor of an 18th-century building that
retains its original wide wooden staircase, which leads up to
his front door. His apartment is testament to his passion for
interiors, as well as his great eye for furniture, curios and art.
It was intended as both a home and a shop, but Oliver has
become so busy with his interior design business that the shop
is now open only on special occasions and at Christmas.

There is an air of grandeur about the apartment – all the original features are still intact, including the tall double doors that open from one room into the next, the soaring windows and the elegant panelling. But Oliver has filled it with a mix of antique and modern, industrial-looking furniture and objects, which creates a edgy, almost theatrical effect.

When Oliver moved into the apartment, the first thing he did was to repaint. The limited colour palette, which includes a soft grey and an old-fashioned dusky pink, is muted and soothing, and works well with the furniture, which is mostly dark wood, dull metal or painted black or grey.

The front door opens directly into a tiny kitchen space, which has been artfully slotted into what was originally an old store cupboard.

BEAUTY AT WORK.
Discreetly incorporated into the shop is Oliver's work space. Items for sale intermingle with office accessories on his desk, its top made of rough untreated wood (previous spread).

ECLECTIC MIX.
Oliver's home is full of treasures, some of which are for sale; there are others he can't bear to part with. The splendid chandelier is casually displayed hanging from a clothes-shop rail (this page).

SPONTANEITY.
Diverse items and pieces of
furniture juxtaposed with one
another give the impression of a
home in a state of flux. From
broken oriental shoulder poles to
an antique framed mirror with
a black cutout making two oval
mirrors, the choice of objects
reflects an appealing spontaneity
(this page).

Size isn't an issue, thanks to the kitchen's clever design, and everything is close to hand. There are a few cabinets for storing china and pots and pans, and Oliver uses an old table as a work surface – a bold contrast to the galvanized shelving unit alongside, which is stacked with everyday china as well as accommodating a microwave oven.

From the kitchen, a narrow corridor leads into the rest of the apartment, which consists of an elegant enfilade of rooms opening one into the next. The first room is the office, which doubles as Oliver's shop. In common with the rest of the apartment, it is spacious and elegant, with worn wooden floorboards full of character. Oliver designed the tall, freestanding shelf units using untreated metal frames and wooden shelves. Constructed to display items for sale, they are objects of beauty in themselves.

UTILITARIAN.
There is not a single comfortable chair in the dining/living room. Oliver says he doesn't need a sofa in order to relax. The centrepiece of the room is the dining table, which is often covered in books and decorative objects, such as this Balinese urn and bowl. The ceiling lamps, made from a metal holder, bulb and fabric-covered cord, add a utilitarian note (this spread).

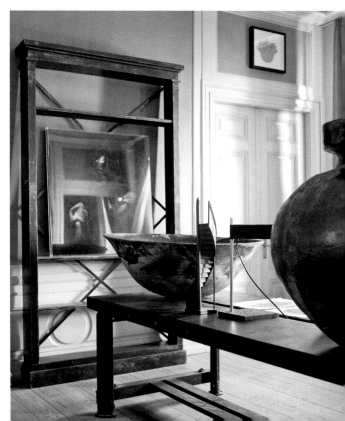

LAID-BACK COLOUR.
The colour scheme in Oliver's uncluttered bedroom, as in other parts of his home, comprises muted tones of grey, black and an old-fashioned dusty pink, creating a haven of tranquillity. The walls are hand-painted by brush for a textured effect. Adding a personal touch to this pared-down space are a still life of Oliver's shoe collection and, piled up on a simple stool, pieces of linen dyed various shades of grey; they have no purpose other than to look gorgeous (this spread).

simple, restful, calm. OLIVER'S BEDROOM CONTAINS JUST THE BARE NECESSITIES: AN ANTIQUE BLACK WOODEN CABINET FOR STORING CLOTHES AND AN UNASSUMING LOW-LEVEL DIVAN BED. THE LOOK EPITOMIZES HIS APPROACH TO HOME DESIGN.

Double doors lead into the dining room/living room, where there is not a comfortable sofa or armchair in sight – Oliver says he can sit just as well in any other chair – and the large metal dining table in the middle of the room is covered in piles of books interspersed with decorative objects. Behind it, reminiscent of museum display cases, are floor-to-ceiling glazed wooden cabinets, home to Oliver's collection of art books, as well as photos, pictures and other treasures.

The last of the three rooms is Oliver's bedroom, which is almost monastic in its simplicity. Storage space for clothes is provided by an antique wooden cabinet, and the bed is an unpretentious low-level divan. The decor epitomizes Oliver's approach to the design of his home. His aim is to create a space that is, above all, restful and calm.

Oliver says that, when he falls in love with a piece, he buys it, regardless of the practical considerations – he found a huge large terracotta urn in Bali, and had it shipped home, where it now enjoys pride of place on his dining table. Oliver is also passionate about art, but he never buys on a whim. All the paintings and objects are given space to breathe, so, although something intriguing or enchanting catches the eye at every turn, the apartment remains a naturally simple, elegant home.

ARTFUL DISPLAYS.
The seat of a battered wooden chair and a folding stool are ideal flat surfaces for displays of, respectively, vintage rulers and a tape measure, and a skein of grey wool (this page).

WALL OF VEGETATION.
In the living room, in contrast to the glistening plastered wall, is a living wall of abundant green vegetation. It must be as close as you can get to nature indoors (opposite).

a green house in the city.

IN THE CENTRE OF PARIS, JEAN-MARC, AN ART PROMOTER, AND HIS WIFE, VIVETTE, A CLOTHES DESIGNER, HAVE BUILT THEIR DREAM HOME. FLANKED ON ALL SIDES BY GRAND 19TH-CENTURY BUILDINGS, IT IS A SPACIOUS, LIGHT-FILLED, FOUR-STOREY HOUSE THAT REVEALS ITS OWNERS' PASSION FOR PLANTS.

The house occupies a small plot of land that was empty when Jean-Marc and Vivette came upon it by chance a few years ago. When they discovered that they could build on the site, they bought it immediately. Taking into account the size of the plot and the surrounding buildings, the couple decided to build up rather than out, creating a tall, light and bright city home.

From the front door, a narrow hallway leads to the sitting room, where the only natural light comes from skylights at one end. The room is dark and cosy, but what sets it apart are three tree trunks positioned in one

corner. Jean-Marc and Vivette found them on site when they bought the land and decided that they were too amazing to lose. Their rough texture offers a contrast to the sleek concrete walls and floor. Simply furnished with low sofas and colourful cushions, this space acts as a temporary art gallery for sculptors invited by the couple to exhibit their work.

A metal staircase leads up to the kitchen/dining area at the back of the house and the living area at the front. The two spaces are divided by a glass and metal lift that connects this floor with the bedrooms upstairs.

With its stainless-steel appliances and and black walls, the kitchen is industrial-modern in style. The polished-concrete floor, reflected in the ceiling of grey concrete slabs, reinforces the contemporary feel. To soften the look, the couple have added an antique sideboard at one end of the kitchen, while at the other end of the room floor-to-ceiling sliding doors lead to a terrace, the first of many outdoor spaces. Here, the mass of foliage associated with an abundance of plants and trees evokes a tropical feel.

The kitchen leads through into a soaring double-height living area, where the big surprise is a luscious, tactile 'growing' wall made up of jungly vegetation in a spectrum of green shades. This is not only a striking decorative feature but also an efficient way to provide insulation and absorb sound, both of which are important in a lofty space full of hard surfaces. The remainder of the room is furnished sparsely, with antique

TEXTURAL INTEREST.
Sheets of vintage coloured paper create an original textural display (above).

ROUGH AND READY.
A banister made from rough planks lines the gallery above the living space, where a chair and an old storage cabinet are used for displays (right and far right).

AT HOME.
Well-worn leather armchairs look at home amid the riot of foliage (opposite).

leather armchairs, a coffee table and an antique wooden table that's used as a desk. On the wall above the desk hangs a very different decorative feature – a precise grid of large sheets of paper printed with poems in golden type, creating a rich and textured effect.

On the top floor, reached by a lift or narrow stairs, is the master bedroom and bathroom plus a guest room. In the bedroom is a large pivoting porthole-style window that overlooks another terrace filled with gently rustling bamboo.

In designing their home, Jean-Marc and Vivette drew inspiration from the architecture of Le Corbusier, whose buildings often featured roof gardens as well as floor-to-ceiling windows. They also wanted to create a home that was in touch with the natural world by cultivating an oasis of tropical greenery in the heart of one of Europe's busiest cities.

COLOUR AND TEXTURE.
Contrasts of colour and texture give character and interest to the kitchen. The black-painted walls and stainless-steel units set a modern tone that's softened by an antique sideboard (opposite and far right). Wooden spoons stand to attention on a shelf (right). The kitchen leads onto the living area, with its glorious living wall (above).

heartfelt messages. ABOVE THE BED, COLOUR-COORDINATED POST-IT NOTES WITH PERSONAL MESSAGES WRITTEN ON THEM HAVE BEEN ARRANGED IN A HEART SHAPE, TO CREATE AN ORIGINAL AND INTIMATE DISPLAY.

LIGHT AND AIRY.
The master bedroom has been very simply decorated and furnished, with only a plain bed and wooden garden chairs, so as not to detract from the huge pivoting window. Leaving the window unadorned ensures that the room is light and airy, while an element of privacy is provided by the plaint containers on the terrace (this spread).

WONDER WALLS.
Most of the walls at la Maison Pujol are still the original stone, which adds life and texture to the interior. The walls are a wonderful backdrop for both modern and vintage furniture as well as the wood-burning stove in the living room (left and far left).

PERFECT MATCH.
In the living area, the original stable floor has been retained. Small, well-worn black cobbles make for an uneven but beautiful surface, complementing the rough concrete and stone walls (opposite).

the old stable.

IN A SMALL VILLAGE CLOSE TO THE FORTIFIED TOWN OF CARCASSONNE IN SOUTH-WEST FRANCE IS LA MAISON PUJOL, AN INTRIGUING B&B. ORIGINALLY A STABLE, THE BUILDING HAS BEEN PAINSTAKINGLY RESTORED BY THE CURRENT OWNERS.

Built as a stable in the 19th-century, La Maison Pujol now incorporates all the modern conveniences and, in its new incarnation as a bed-and-breakfast place, offers extremely comfortable guest accommodation. The owners, Aurélie and René, live here too, on the second floor of the building, which has its own entrance at the back of the house. This has the advantage of giving the couple, as well as their guests, some privacy.

From the outset, the couple were determined to retain as many of the building's original features as possible. Part of the ground floor has been converted into the living and breakfast area for bed-and-breakfast guests, but minimal changes have been made – just

some necessary restoration to make the space appear fresh and inviting. Combined with the muted and calming colours of the walls and furnishings, the highly unusual cobblestone floor – which is made up of small, irregular black stones smoothed and polished by the passage of time – creates an overall effect that is breathtakingly beautiful.

In the living area, most of the rough stone walls have been left exposed, while others have been covered with a smooth layer of concrete. The wooden ceiling beams have also been left exposed and painted white to introduce more light into the interior. Two modern dark brown leather sofas have a lustrous sheen that perfectly complements the subtle gloss of the polished cobblestone floor. This space is also home to a iron wood-burning stove, which keeps it snug and cosy during the winter months.

The living area leads through to the breakfast room, where a long, plain wooden table takes pride of place. Above the table, hanging from jointed metal rods, are a row of lights with cylindrical fabric shades, one in a unexpectedly vibrant tone of red that provides a welcome splash of colour.

Beyond the breakfast area is a small and functional industrial-style kitchen, with sleek lines and modern materials that provide something of a contrast to the rest of the interior. The glossy stainless-steel units and appliances are offset by a large kitchen island made of wood and equipped with traditional wicker baskets and drawers that offer plenty of storage space. The original stone

floor has been replaced with one of polished concrete, which is easier to clean and maintain.

Slightly uneven white-painted stone stairs lead up to the five guest bedrooms. Each one has been individually but simply decorated and furnished, combining both vintage and modern pieces, such as old wooden stools and funky plastic chairs, for added interest and personality. Some of these rooms still have their original bare

IN CONTRAST.
The wire Bertoia chairs and cylindrical lampshades suspended from metal rods bring a contemporary touch to the breakfast room, with its original stone floor and roughly finished walls. Stainless-steel units also gives the kitchen a modern feel, but the central wooden island with its wicker baskets prevents it from looking too starkly industrial (left and above).

CONTEMPORARY EDGE.
A limited colour palette has been
used in the living area, which
accentuates the different textures
in the room – ancient stone, whitewashed wood and smooth leather.

simple success. PLACING EMPHASIS ON TEXTURE AND KEEPING THE COLOUR PALETTE LIMITED GIVES A SIMPLICITY TO THE GUEST ROOMS AND MAKES THEM TRANQUIL AND WELCOMING RETREATS.

stone walls visible. Elsewhere, layers of old paint and concrete have been left intact, while other walls have been plastered and painted for a more finished effect. All the bedrooms have white-painted wooden floors to convey a feeling of freshness and light, and each room has its own simple but indulgent ensuite bathroom, flatteringly lit and decorated in calming hues. Vintage furniture, such as traditional wooden benches and antique wooden ladders to hold towels, offsets the contemporary styling.

One thing that is particularly pleasing about La Maison Pujol is the way in which the owners have lavished love and care upon its restoration, respecting the building's history and retaining

original elements wherever possible. Even though the stable building has been sensitively updated for modern-day living, it is still possible to appreciate the traditional skills used in its construction. I believe that a building's original features should be kept for future generations to enjoy, and there is a great abundance of such features here.

SAME BUT DIFFERENT.
Although the guest bedrooms have all been decorated and furnished slightly differently, they share a discreet and tranquil atmosphere. Like the bedrooms, the ensuite bathrooms are simply decorated with a contemporary edge (this spread).

EVERYTHING IN ITS PLACE.
Many of the decorative objects that Jacques has acquired have ended up in his studio. It is a creative mix where nothing seems out of place (opposite).

TURNING GREEN.
A simple tap, made from copper piping, has started to oxidize and looks perfect in its location (right).

WORK DESK.
This large glass-topped desk with wooden legs has been designed especially for making photographic prints (far right).

the converted church.

I HAVE ALWAYS LONGED TO LIVE IN AN OLD CHURCH, SO, WHEN I READ ABOUT THIS CONVERSION IN ARLES IN THE SOUTH OF FRANCE, I JUST HAD TO SEE IT FOR MYSELF TO MARVEL AT THE CHANGES THAT HAD BEEN WROUGHT. ALTHOUGH THE EXTERIOR IS STILL THAT OF AN 18TH-CENTURY CHURCH, MOST OF THE INTERIOR HAS BEEN TRANSFORMED BEYOND RECOGNITION. JACQUES, THE OWNER, A PSYCHOANALYST AND ARTIST, HAS CREATED A HOME AND WORK SPACE THAT IS AMAZINGLY MODERN, WARM AND LIVEABLE – AND COMPLETELY UNIQUE.

Access to the four floors of the church is either via an open staircase or an old lift, which was installed when the church was used as a warehouse in the 1940s. The lift is particularly useful after shopping trips, when groceries need to be transported upstairs, or when Jacques has a sudden urge to redecorate or move the furniture around from floor to floor.

With dazzling views over the rooftops of Arles and the countryside lying beyond, the top floor resembles an enormous, open-plan loft space. Natural light floods in from skylights above, as well as through large French windows that open onto a terrace. Virtually all the walls have been left untouched, with the ancient stone on show, creating a beautiful and varied backdrop.

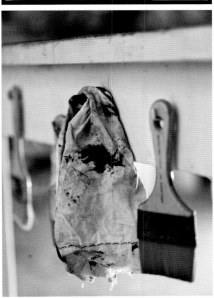

PRESERVING HISTORY.
Stone walls in the studio are
a constant reminder of the
building's history. The vintage
basket is the ideal place for
storing rolls of old posters
and paper (previous spread).

CREATIVE SPACE.
Jacques's work studio takes
up the entire first floor. It is
an evolving space, conducive
to creativity (this spread).

organic decoration. A HOME OR ROOM DOES NOT HAVE TO BE
PLANNED ACCORDING TO ANY RULES OF DESIGN AND DECORATION
BUT SHOULD COME INTO BEING THROUGH AN ORGANIC PROCESS.

In the kitchen, however, Jacques has had the stone walls plastered and painted to make them easier to clean and maintain, although the wooden ceiling and beams, with their wonderful patina of age, have been left exposed to showcase the church's original construction. Jacques wanted the building to bear witness to the passage of time as well as being an efficient modern home.

Jacques designed the kitchen himself, choosing worktops constructed from local stone. It's a simple, user-friendly space. With entertaining in mind, he installed two sinks side by side and has kept most of the storage open. Old fruit boxes provide attractive and easily accessible (not to mention inexpensive) additional storage underneath the sinks. A custom-built wooden cabinet has a fittingly ecclesiastical air about it and is used to store glassware and china within easy reach of the dining table. The whole space is very convivial. Positioning the dining table close to the kitchen work area allows Jacques

LIVED-IN KITCHEN.
The kitchen on the top floor was designed by Jacques. He loves to entertain, which accounts for the lived-in feel of the space. Kitchen accessories are placed on open shelves or in the fruit boxes underneath the sinks (opposite).

DINING IN STYLE.
The antique dining table and Thonet bentwood chairs take centre stage in the kitchen. Placed conveniently close to the table is a cupboard used for storing china and glassware (this page).

mixing old and new. THE KITCHEN/DINING AREA SUCCESSFULLY COMBINES OLD AND NEW, WITH THE DIFFERENT MATERIALS GIVING THE SPACE A VERY NATURAL FEEL.

to chat to guests while cooking, or guests to help out if necessary. Classic Thonet bentwood chairs in different designs flank the antique table. Jacques unearthed these at various flea markets and has now amassed quite a collection.

Scouring fleamarkets is one of Jacques's greatest pleasures and, over the years, he has amassed an impressive collection of treasures, from birdcages and books to antique linens and frames. In the adjacent living area, an antique table acts as a display case for the latest pieces to catch his eye. As Jacques makes new purchases so the display changes to accommodate new favourites, but nothing ever seems to get thrown away. Fortunately, lack of space is not an issue!

In front of the table, roomy antique leather armchairs for reading and relaxation add to the laidback atmosphere. Behind the only dividing wall, on the top floor, are the master bedroom and bathroom. In these simply furnished rooms, the bare, undecorated walls maintain the same natural feel throughout.

On the first floor is Jacques's studio, where he creates photographic prints using an alternative printing process called resinopigmentype. He uses old maps, antique papers and even antique fabrics to print on, with the result that the finished work, which is displayed all around the church, looks as though it belongs to the space and always has done. Wall shelves are filled

with more flea-market finds and books, clustered together in a haphazard and spontaneous mix. An expansive work table is at the heart of the studio and around it are a scattering of chairs and smaller tables, randomly positioned to give the space a natural, unstaged feel. Not a thing appears contrived or out of place. A home or a room does not have to be planned according to any rules of decorating but should naturally evolve, and this is exactly what has happened in this very successfully converted church.

FLEA-MARKET FINDS.
The living area is an interesting mix of plants and decorative items found at flea markets. One of Jacques's photographic prints forms part of the esoteric display on the antique wooden table. The old leather armchairs are ideal for an afternoon nap (this spread).

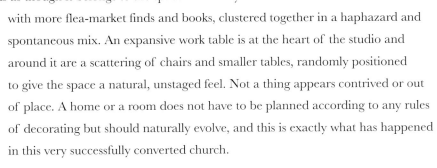

MASTER BEDROOM.
The master bedroom has the same spontaneous feel as the rest of the converted church, with the bare stone walls complementing the wooden furniture and natural linen bed covers (opposite).

STUDIO PIECES.
In spite of their age differences and style, the desk chair in the studio appears completely at home with the vintage rattan lounger behind it (this page).

TEXTURE AND COMFORT.
The pile of throws in shades of brown and grey adds texture to an otherwise plain, pared-down space (far left).

ADDING PERSONALITY.
A simple bench and a set of family photos on a tongue-and-groove wall introduce personality to an austure and narrow hallway (left).

SIMPLE ELEGANCE.
Oversized armchairs and a sofa in white loose covers take centre stage in the living room, with an old rustic bench serving as a coffee table (opposite).

naturally relaxed.

REINI AND GERARD LIVE IN A SMALL VILLAGE IN THE FLAT, OPEN COUNTRYSIDE KNOWN AS 'BIRDLAND' IN THE NORTH OF HOLLAND. DESPITE THE PEACE AND QUIET OF THEIR SURROUNDINGS, THEY ARE ONLY A 35-MINUTE DRIVE FROM AMSTERDAM. BOTH OF THEM WORK FROM HOME: REINI, A FORMER STYLIST, NOW CONCENTRATES ON REDECORATING OTHER PEOPLE'S HOUSES, WHILE GERARD IS A RETAIL DESIGNER.

There came a time when Reini and Gerard realized their home was no longer big enough to accommodate both their growing family and their home offices. The solution was either to move to a larger house or to extend their current house to create more space. They chose the second option simply because they loved their home so much.

The couple had very clear ideas about how the two-storey extension should look. They wanted it to blend imperceptibly with the old house, and this aim has been achieved. When you look at the facade, it's almost impossible to distinguish between the old and the new parts of the building. Both are clad in the same brick, and the new windows follow the design of the earlier ones. Inside, the only difference is that the new living room on the ground floor has a taller ceiling, to admit more light and to make the space appear larger.

There is something Shaker-like about this home. It is simply decorated, with natural materials and a limited palette: grey and white with touches of wood.

shaker style. THE PARED-DOWN LOOK OF THE LIVING ROOM RECALLS THE STYLE OF THE SHAKERS, WHO BELIEVED THAT EVERY OBJECT SHOULD BE WELL CHOSEN AND HAVE A PRACTICAL USE.

PANORAMIC VIEWS.
The tall sash windows have been left unadorned to make the most of the panoramic views. Wide floorboards, identical to those in the original part of the house, have been laid in the living room, helping to unite the old and new (opposite).

OPEN FIREPLACE.
Smoke stains from the open fireplace climb the white-painted wall but no attempt has been made to remove them, which only adds to the natural feel of the room The stool was made by the Dutch designer Piet Hein (this page).

DUAL PURPOSE.
The living room doubles as a dining room. Its long wooden table is brought into use when the kitchen table isn't big enough. Reini and Gerard store their impressive magazine collection in piles lining the walls, while a vintage wooden bench is covered with books. A steep, wide ladder leads to the new upper floor (this spread).

With such a simple backdrop, it is easy to introduce colour in the shape of decorative objects or art without the interior feeling too busy or crowded.

In the new part of the building is a repositioned front door leading into a hallway. Custom-made floor-to-ceiling cabinets, useful for tidying away shoes, line the walls. One door opens onto the new living area, while another leads to the original hallway and, beyond, to the kitchen, master bedroom and bathroom, and Reini's office.

The kitchen, at the back of the house, has a glorious view over the garden and to the fields beyond. It was designed by Reini and Gerard, and has custom-made worktops and cabinets. Due to the sloping ceiling there was no room for wall cabinets, so they devoted the one full-height wall to

CONTEMPORARY EDGE.
The kitchen table has
a rustic quality. Like the
custom-made floor-to-
ceiling cupboards, it
is made out of planks
of wood. Giving a
contemporary edge are
the large industrial-style
lamps and moulded-
plastic chairs in various
colours (this page).

COMBINATION.
A winning combination
of different materials is
evident in the kitchen.
The modern concrete
worktops and stainless-
steel oven are softened
by the wooden cabinet
doors and hood for the
cooker. Plain white tiles
make a fittingly neutral
backdrop (opposite).

floor-to-ceiling cupboards painted white. Elsewhere, they fitted base cabinets in natural wood. Taking centre stage is a large wooden kitchen table, perfect for family gatherings.

Across from the kitchen is Reini's office. The tools of her trade – a computer and a sewing machine – are placed on a large wooden table beneath a tall window. When the sun streams in, this is a particularly inviting spot. Along the corridor is the master bedroom and the bathroom. With windows on two sides, the white-painted bedroom is light and bright. Clever storage has been built in, with floor-to-ceiling wardrobes and a window seat with cupboards beneath.

Presenting a complete contrast is the master bathroom, which is tiled from top to bottom in dramatic black slate.

A staircase leads up from the old hallway to the guest bedrooms and bathroom on the first floor. These rooms are sparingly but elegantly furnished, with the walls covered in white-painted tongue-and-groove panelling.

On the ground floor, the new living room doubles as a dining room, with an antique wooden table for occasions when there are more guests than can be seated in the kitchen. With windows on three sides and doors leading to the garden, this room is also flooded with light. The room is simply furnished, with a huge white sofa and armchairs. The open fireplace is unadorned, in tune with the pared-down decorative theme.

Ladder steps lead from the living room to the new part of the upper storey, which contains Gerard's office and the grandchildren's room. On one wall are custom-made floor-to-ceiling cupboards with doors made from recycled pieces of wood. The doors fold open like window shutters and conceal cosy beds – an ingenious idea, which I'm sure the grandchildren love.

Reini and Gerard's home is beautiful and unfussy but extremely comfortable at the same time. Their attention to detail means that the extension is perfectly in keeping with the original house, both inside and out. And by doubling the floor space they have made sure that they can live and work here with absolute ease.

IN THE ROOF.
One of the guest rooms is tucked away under the slanted ceiling of the roof. The room is far from gloomy though, with its white-painted tongue-and-groove walls and light-coloured bed linen (above).

ROOM WITH A VIEW.
Placed by a window, Reini's office desk, where she works on her interior designs, has a wonderfully generous supply of natural light, as well as an inspirational view over the garden and street (right).

HIDEAWAYS.
When the grandchildren come to stay, they sleep in beds that are concealed behind hinged doors made of reclaimed wooden slats. It is a traditional idea that the children adore. The rest of the space is a play area. The ladder leads up the loft (opposite).

FLOODED WITH LIGHT.
The kitchen/dining area is beautifully light, thanks to the large paned windows at the front of the house (opposite).

PILED HIGH.
A simple still life of stacked books and boxes creates personality in a corner of the kitchen (far left).

BOTTOM HEAVY.
An oversized and lopsided pottery jug has two roles – as the decorative home for a colchicum bulb and as a practical book end (left).

simply natural.

STELLA AND TIM LIVE ON A NARROW, TREE-LINED STREET IN THE CENTRE OF AMSTERDAM. TALL AND NARROW, THE COUPLE'S HOUSE IS VERY TYPICAL OF THE AREA. THERE IS A VILLAGEY FEEL TO THIS HISTORIC PART OF THE CITY, WITH ITS WINDING COBBLED STREETS AND NETWORK OF CANALS.

When you enter this relaxed, comfortable house, it comes as no surprise to learn that Stella works in interior design for an international clothing company. Tim is a restaurateur, and his restaurant, around the corner from the house, has been designed and decorated by the couple in the same contemporary but soothing, natural style as their home.

Like their neighbours, Stella and Tim have plants at the entrance to their house. They have also added a small bench, which increases the sense of welcome and is a lovely spot for enjoying a morning coffee.

Once inside, the kitchen/dining area has a minimal, contemporary feel. With a large window looking onto the street and another overlooking a tiny courtyard, the space is light and airy. Light streaming in through the windows is reflected in the polished concrete floor. Mismatched dining chairs, stools and a long antique bench surround a simple dining table with metal legs. The pale wood of the bench and table add to the contemporary feel.

Built-in cupboards and drawers with stainless-steel fronts run the length of the wall opposite, providing

ON DISPLAY.
The wall above the kitchen units is home to a display of Stella's photographs (right).

EASY REACH.
Open shelves provide additional storage within easy reach for everyday items and help keep the worksurfaces free from clutter (below).

SLEEK STEEL.
The fitted units with stainless-steel fronts give a professional look to the kitchen. The custom-built worktops, made of polished concrete, are deeper than the base cabinets to provide more work space. Kitchen utensils are kept close to hand in an antique soup tureen (opposite).

plenty of space for cooking and storage. These are supplemented by chunky open shelves, which lighten the atmosphere. The stainless steel imparts a modern edge to the space and contrasts with the traditional sash windows. The custom-made work surface is crafted from polished concrete and extends beyond the length of the base cabinets, to create an additional area for food preparation. A grid of framed pictures taken by Stella hangs above the cabinets, revealing her passion for photography. The white-painted walls here, and throughout the house, are the perfect neutral backdrop.

An open staircase leads up to the living space on the first floor. The room is simply furnished, with comfy seating for relaxing and watching television. The sofa resembles a day bed and is covered in a slubby vintage French linen. Heaps of cushions in muted shades from grey to fawn increase the comfort levels. Customized shelving provides

SIT BACK AND RELAX.
The sofa is an old mattress covered in vintage linen and heaped with scatter cushions (opposite).

SENSIBLE STORAGE.
Chunky shelves in the living room make the most of the dead space in the recess, providing storage for books and collectables (right). Similar use has been made of the recess in Stella's office, where space is at a premium (above). The antique desk, meanwhile, provides characterful storage (below).

ordered storage and display spaces for books, family photographs and collectables. It's the perfect place to hang out.

Another flight of stairs takes you up to the second floor, where the guest room and home office are located. As elsewhere, everything is spick and span, with books kept close to hand on fitted shelves, and papers and documents filed away in boxes. Above the desk hangs a cluster of framed photographs of friends, family and trips she and Tim have taken together.

Follow the stairs up one more flight, and you reach the top floor and Stella and Tim's bedroom and en suite bathroom. In keeping with the rest of the house, the bedroom is simply decorated, with

little more than a bed, dressed with linen sheets in dusty pastel hues, and two metal bedside tables. In the bathroom, the wooden sink set in a custom-made unit was originally an old trough that held animal feed. The open shelves beneath are piled high with towels, while attractive boxes keep more mundane bathroom paraphernalia out of sight.

The house has been through many structural changes. When Stella first moved in 12 years ago, she was sharing the house with friends. When they moved out and Tim moved in, the couple rejigged the layout to make it workable and comfortable for the two of them. Slowly but surely, they set about replacing stairs, moving walls and adding rooms, and now, nine years later, their home is just as they want it: functional and contemporary, but with a relaxed, personal touch.

back to basics. PARED DOWN TO THE BARE ESSENTIALS AND
DECORATED IN A NEUTRAL PALETTE, THE MASTER BEDROOM IS
A HAVEN OF CALM AT THE TOP OF THE HOUSE.

BARE NECESSITIES.
Pillows in soothing tones of grey and
beige and dark side tables break up
the expanse of white in the sparsely
furnished master bedroom. The
en suite bathroom is just as simply
decorated, with open storage and a
custom-made wooden sink. Hanging
from the ceiling in the guest room is
a 1960s rattan chair, with a sheepskin
rug; a perfect spot for reading a book.
On the wall facing the staircase,
wooden letters spell out the obvious
(this spread).

ATMOSPHERIC COLOUR.
A restricted colour scheme is used to great effect in Monique Mejk's home. Here, lichen-covered twigs, nubbly fabrics and carved wooden candlesticks are combined to create scenes reminiscent of an oil painting (this spread).

DOG TIRED.
The decor makes this large living room feel cosy even when the fire is not lit. The warm brown-grey linen of the armchair matches the walls. Oscar the dog sleeps comfortably in his antique wooden bed (overleaf).

shades of grey.

IN AN OLD DUTCH HOUSE IN A SMALL VILLAGE BY A RIVER, ABOUT AN HOUR'S DRIVE FROM AMSTERDAM, MONIQUE MEJK LIVES WITH HER HUSBAND AND THEIR TWO TEENAGE CHILDREN. MONIQUE'S PASSION IS FOR INTERIORS AND SHE HAS SET UP A SHOP ON THE GROUND FLOOR OF THE HOUSE SELLING FURNITURE AND DECORATIVE OBJECTS, BOTH NEWLY DESIGNED AND ANTIQUE. SHE ALSO HELPS OTHERS TO DECORATE AND FURNISH THEIR HOMES.

As might be expected, Monique is fond of redesigning her own home on a regular basis. And, with the shop literally on her doorstep, she finds it difficult to resist the temptation to 'borrow' new items and carry them up the narrow staircase to the living quarters above. Monique is also an accomplished artist, and her portraits and nudes are displayed in the shop as well as throughout her home.

Monique's unique sense of style is apparent both in the furniture she sources for her shop and in the way she has decorated her home. It is also evident in her paintings. She is drawn to a muted palette, particularly shades of grey, which is one of her favourite colours.

Although Monique usually repaints the interior of her village house frequently, the charcoal shade on the walls has been left untouched for some time. She feels

quite comfortable with this colour, as does the rest of the
family, although her husband likes to joke that one day she
will wake up to a wall that he has painted red!

The shop, also painted charcoal grey, has large windows
both front and back, so, even though the colour scheme is
moody, the space feels light. A staircase leads up to the first
floor, home to the kitchen/dining area and living room.

The living space is painted a velvety dark charcoal but,
as in the shop, the space nevertheless feels bright because of
the abundance of light that comes through the tall windows.
Muted tones feature in the soft furnishings as well as the
paintwork, and texture is all-important here: the deep sofa
and armchairs are covered in a brown-grey washed linen,
while the dark walls have an almost powdery bloom to them.

The room is largely furnished with antique finds, but there are a few exceptions. The coffee table, for example, is one of Monique's own designs. Constructed out of an old wooden door, it has metal legs, which bring a raw, industrial edge to the piece. Monique is inspired by nature, and twigs and boughs in large terracotta urns are carefully arranged in every room.

The custom-made kitchen was designed by Monique and is painted a grey so dark that at first glance it appears to be black. Contrasting textures abound. The concrete work surfaces have a dull gleam, while the cabinet doors are crafted from broad wooden planks. At one end of the room, surrounding the antique dining table, is a group of mismatching chairs and low Chinese wooden stools, together with a high-backed sofa upholstered in pearly grey-suede. Propped up against the brick wall behind are

DINNER TIME.
In the evenings, the metal chandelier casts a subdued light over the antique dining table. The unusual high-backed upholstered sofa makes the space particularly inviting. The wall behind the sofa has been left in its original state (above and opposite).

STILL LIFE.
Old chopping boards and dried branches in a terracotta urn have been arranged to make long-lasting displays (right and far right).

THE KITCHEN.
The kitchen units, designed by
Monique, have wooden doors
painted a very dark grey, creating
a pleasing contrast with the
unpainted wooden floorboards.
The stone sink and concrete
worktops introduce different
texture, as do the ceramic plates
and the bowl piled high with
walnuts picked during a country
walk (this page and opposite).

bare minimum. FROM THE FURNITURE AND PAINTWORK TO THE SOFT FURNISHINGS AND
DECORATIVE OBJECTS, THE COLOURS USED THROUGHOUT HAVE BEEN KEPT TO THE BARE
MINIMUM, WITH SHADES OF GREY, BROWN AND GREEN PREDOMINATING.

LAID-BACK CHARM.

The chaise longue is the only piece
of furniture in the master bedroom.
The frayed edge of the loose cover
is deliberate, adding to the effect of
laid-back charm. Soft cushions and
throws contribute still further to the
sense of relaxation, as does bed linen
in natural shades (below and opposite).

GLOSSY GREYS.

The bathroom is painted a dark
anthracite-grey. A simple display of
pretty embossed soaps on an antique
wooden stool introduces softness and
texture (right and far right).

a number of Monique's paintings. This wall is the only one
that has been left in its original state, to preserve just a little
piece of the history of the house.

From the living/kitchen space, another set of stairs leads
to the master bedroom and bathroom. Painted her trademark
grey, the bedroom is elegantly minimal with an intriguing
variety of textures. Three antique wooden doors have been
adapted to make a headboard, while traditional wicker
baskets have become bedside tables. The only other piece
of furniture is a linen-covered chaise longue by the fireplace.

Across the hallway is the bathroom, also designed by
Monique. Ever practical, she included a shower as well as
a bathtub and two basins to make the morning rush less
stressful. Although more streamlined and contemporary in
style than the rest of house, the bathroom fits in seamlessly.
The walls have been simply plastered then painted black.

Monique's home has an absolutely distinctive character.
The sombre colour palette is enlivened by clever use of
contrasting textures and dreamy, imaginative displays. The
dark, sparsely furnished interior has the serene atmosphere
of a Dutch painting from the golden age and is inviting and
soothing for the soul as well as the eyes.

FADED WITH TIME.
Antique framed etchings, paintings and memorabilia blend beautifully with the faded wallpaper (opposite).

BEHIND THE SCENES.
On top of the antique grey cabinet in Pascale's atelier is her collection of old tailors' mannequins (far left).

WELCOMING DISPLAYS.
Impressive pieces of antique furniture help to make up the displays in the hallway, which include an armchair dwarfed by an enormous glass bowl (left).

in search of lost time.

LOCATED IN A GRAND 18TH-CENTURY HOUSE IN THE HEART OF AVIGNON IS VOX POPULI, A DELIGHTFUL AND COMPLETELY UNIQUE INTERIORS SHOP OWNED AND RUN BY PASCALE AND BRUNO. WHEN YOU ENTER THE LARGE HALLWAY FROM THE NARROW STREET, YOU FEEL AS IF YOU ARE STEPPING BACK IN TIME.

This house has belonged to the same family since the time it was built. Amazingly, the interior has remained untouched for almost 100 years, and it provides a fantastical backdrop to the creations of Pascale and Bruno, which are on sale in the 'shop' on the ground floor. In appearance, Vox Populi is as far removed from a shop as could be imagined. Instead, it has been furnished as if it were a private home and filled with all manner of intriguing objects – from handmade wirework sculptures and chandeliers to stuffed dogs and cushions – giving the space a very personal touch.

Pascale and Bruno have decorated the shop's front room to resemble a cosy dining room, and the look is so authentic that you almost feel as if supper is about to be served. A large table is surrounded by antique upholstered chairs and covered with decorative fabric chihuahuas and attractive wirework cages, designed and made by Pascale.

The wirework, for which the shop is celebrated, is very fine and detailed, with something of a fairytale quality to it. Along the walls, other pieces of wirework for sale are displayed in large cupboards.

From the 'dining room', large French double doors lead into the 'living room', where two sofas face each other and an antique coffee table stands between them. Here, the couple showcase soft linen cushions with printed patterns and more examples of their wirework, including table as well as ceiling chandeliers, made by Bruno. There are no windows, but the room is artfully lit by the chandeliers and wirework cages, which have small lamps inside them, to create an intimate atmosphere. The beautifully aged wallpaper gives the room an overall colour of soft grey with touches of faded gold.

At the back of the house is Pascale's atelier, where, seated at the large work table in the middle of the room, she twists and bends lengths of wire to create her unique sculptures, ranging from cages and typewriters to glasses and cutlery. This is intricate work that requires a great deal of time, precision and commitment.

LIKE A LIVING ROOM.
The middle room of the ground-floor shop has been arranged to resemble a living room. Two white sofas, with scatter cushions made by Pascale and Bruno, face each other, separated by a mirrored coffee table. Perched on an original radiator, on simple metal stands, is a collection of delicate lace antique clothing (previous spread).

PORTRAIT GALLERY.
Oil portraits hang above the ornate sideboard. One turned to the wall is a backdrop for a dainty wall sconce (this page).

NEW ROLE.
No longer used for its original purpose, the large dining table, covered in antique cotton and linen tablecloths, is now a display surface for the couple's creations (opposite).

Running along one wall in the atelier is a bank of grey-painted cupboards, which are practical as well as attractive. Pascale uses them to store the fabrics, feathers, old beads and buttons that she hunts down in flea markets and uses in her wirework. The back wall, meanwhile, is entirely glass – and original to the building – with a geometric pattern of green and yellow diamonds. Natural light floods into the room through this wall and the skylights above, making this an ideal environment for such complex work.

Pascale and Bruno are also passionate about vintage finds and antiques, and they have amassed diverse collections that are on display throughout the house, including vintage fabrics, tailors' mannequins and glass domes. Pascale uses the domes to display individual pieces, creating original and interesting still lifes.

An impressive stone staircase leads from the hallway to the first floor, where two other rooms have been converted into workshops. In one, Pascale puts the finishing

PEELING PAINT.
This chest of tiny drawers has been left in its original colour. Some of the paint has peeled off to produce a beautiful texture and patina. The wallpapered panel adds another texture, as well as conveying a sense of history (previous spread).

CABINET OF CURIOSITIES.
Pascale's atelier, where she stores flea-market finds and executes her intricate wirework, is a cabinet of curiosities. Nearly every surface is covered (this page).

lovingly hand-made. SEATED AT A LARGE TABLE IN THE MIDDLE OF THE ATELIER, PASCALE TWISTS AND BENDS LENGTHS OF WIRE TO CREATE HER HIGHLY DISTINCTIVE SCULPTURES.

MODERN NECESSITIES.
Computers and a moulded plastic chair give the
ground-floor office a more contemporary look
than the rest of the house, but, as elsewhere, many
of the original features are still intact (this page).

MAKING CHANDELIERS.
Bruno's chandelier workshop is an inspiring space.
Hanging on one wall are pieces of wire bent into
beautiful sinuous shapes, ready, one day, to form
part of a chandelier (opposite).

touches to all the wirework pieces, while the second is where Bruno
makes his signature chandeliers. Suspended from the ceiling in
Bruno's workshop is an array of such chandeliers in the making.

I have always secretly dreamed of finding an original untouched
house, where everything, including the decoration, has been left
intact, so you can imagine how incredible it was for me to be able to
visit and photograph this 18th-century house. The sense of history
here is overwhelming, and the atmosphere that Pascale and Bruno
have created in their shop is completely in tune with the character
and age of a building that is so steeped in the past.

source directory

IN THE UK

APPLEY HOARE ANTIQUES

+44 (0)790 167 5050

appley@appleyhoare.com

Good quality vintage French linen.

BAILEYS HOME AND GARDEN

Whitecross Farm

Bridstow

Herefordshire

HR9 6JU

+44 (0)1989 561931

www.baileyshomeandgarden.
com

*Old French apple crates and
salvage-style shelving for storage,
old wooden shoe lasts and sock
forms, linen-covered sofas and
vintage-style utilitarian
kitchenware.*

BEYOND FRANCE

+44 (0)1285 641867

www.beyondfrance.co.uk

*Vintage European linen
tablecloths, sheets and dyed linen
(in shades of grey) by the metre.*

CARAVAN

3 Redchurch Street

London

E2 7DJ

+44 (0)20 7033 3532

www.caravanstyle.com

*A selection of quirky, vintage-
inspired decorative pieces.*

FARROW & BALL

www.farrow-ball.com

*A broad spectrum of paint colours
with great depth and beauty.*

HOWIE & BELLE

52 Chamberlayne Road

London NW10 3JH

+44 (0)208 964 4553

www.howieandbelle.com

*Eclectic collection of vintage
mirrors, pictures, furniture and
decorative objects, including glass
domes and display cabinets.*

LABOUR AND WAIT

85 Redchurch Street

London

E2 7DJ

+44 (0)20 7729 6253

www.labourandwait.co.uk

*Vintage-inspired hardware,
including old-fashioned enameled
kitchenware and simple utilitarian
French glassware.*

LIBERTY

Great Marlborough Street

London

W1B 5AH

+44 (0)20 7734 1234

www.liberty.co.uk

*Linen and patterned textiles, as
well as a carefully edited selection
of antique furniture.*

PIMPERNEL & PARTNERS

596 Kings Road

London

SW6 2DX

+44 (0)20 7731 2448

www.pimpernelandpartners.
co.uk

*19th-century calico-covered
vintage French furniture and
modern reproductions.*

ARCHITECTURAL ANTIQUES

LASSCO

www.lassco.co.uk

*Architectural salvage in London
and Oxfordshire.*

RETROUVIOUS

www.retrouvious.com

*London-based architectural
salvage company. Their warehouse
is a treasure trove of salvaged
pieces as well as cushions made
from vintage fabrics by Kirsten
Hecktermann. Interior design
projects also undertaken.*

SALVOWEB

www.salvoweb.com

*Online directory of architectural
salvage suppliers, antiques, and
reclaimed materials.*

ANTIQUES AND FLEA MARKETS

IACF

International Antiques &
Collectors Fair

P.O. Box 100, Newark

Nottinghamshire NG24 1DJ

+44 (0)1636 702326

www.iacf.co.uk

*Organizers of regular UK antique
fairs, including those at Newark
(Notts), Swinderby (Lincs),
Shepton Mallet (Somerset) and
Goodwood (West Sussex). Also
see www.antiques-atlas.com and
www.artefact.co.uk for more
information.*

IN EUROPE

L'ARROSAGE

80 rue Oberkampf

75011 Paris

*The most wonderful flower shop,
with a lot of unexpected plants.*

BRANDSTATIONEN

Krukmakargatan 22

11851 Stockholm

*Great shop for vintage accessories
and furniture.*

BROC'MARTEL

12 rue Martel

75010 Paris

www.brocmartel.com

*A small shop with vintage and
industrial furniture and objects.*

DUSTY DECO
Kocksgatan 23
11624 Stockholm
www.dustydeco.com
The best shop for vintage in Sweden, specializes in American vintage and antique furniture and accessories.

EMERY ET CIE
27 Rue de l'Hopital
1000 Brussels
+32 2 513 58 92
www.emeryetcie.com
Wallpapers, furniture, tiles and paint in a spectrum of natural shades from Belgian architect and designer Agnes Emery. Visit their website for details of their shops in Antwerp and Paris. In London, Emery et Cie can be found at Retrouvius (see above).

GARBO INTERIORS
Brahegatan 21
11437 Stockholm
www.garbointeriors.com
Sells vintage and antique furniture and accessories, mostly French.

MARCHÉ AUX PUCES
www.marchesauxpuces.fr
www.parispuces.com
Supposedly the largest antiques market in the world and certainly the most famous flea market in Paris. Here I find inspiration.

Visit Marche Vernaison for smaller objects (99 Rue des Rosiers) and Marche Paul Bert for furniture (96 Rue des Rosiers). Market open Saturday–Monday.

MERCI
111 boulevard Beaumarchais
75003 Paris
+33 1 42 77 00 33
www.merci-merci.com
Concept shop with clothes, homeware and stationery.

L'OBJET QUI PARLE
86 rue des Martyrs
75018 Paris
www.objetquiparle.com
My all-time favourite shop in Paris, where I always find vintage objects for my home and work.

ATELIER 154
154 rue Oberkampf
75011 Paris
+33 6 62 32 79 06
www.atelier154.com
Antique and vintage objects and furniture, mostly industrial.

VOX POPULI
17 rue Thiers
84000 Avignon
+33 4 90 85 70 25
Vintage pieces as well as handcrafted decorative items, lamps and jewellery.

IN THE USA
MODERN VINTAGE SHOPPING
ANTHROPOLOGIE
www.anthropologie.com
Quirky homewares with a vintage spin. Stores across North America and Canada and now in the UK.

ABC CARPET AND HOME
www.abchome.com
Vintage and antique finds, as well as decorative accents. Stores in Manhattan, the Bronx, New Jersey and Florida.

JOHN DERIAN DRY GOODS
10 East Second Street
New York, NY 10003
(+1) 212 677 8408
www.johnderian.com
Classic furniture upholstered in natural linen plus inspiring antiques, quirky prints and home accessories.

MICHELE VARIAN
27 Howard Street
New York, NY 10013
(+1) 212 226 1076
www.michelevarian.com
Industrial-style vintage furniture, lighting, curios and ceramics.

RESTORATION HARDWARE
www.restorationhardware.com
Vintage-washed Belgian linen bedding in natural shades as well as refurbished antiques and vintage reproductions. Leather trunks, metal tables and grain sack-style linen cushions. Stores across the US.

ANTIQUE AND FLEA MARKETS
The USA hosts a wealth of thrift stores and markets. Check their websites for locations and dates. For comprehensive state-by-state flea market directories, visit www.fleausa.com and www.fleamarketguide.com.

CALIFORNIA
Rose Bowl Flea Market
www.rgcshows.com

MASSACHUSETTS
Brimfield Antiques Show
www.brimfieldshow.com

NEW JERSEY
Englishtown Auction Sales
www.englishtownauction.com

NEW YORK
Hell's Kitchen Flea Market
www.hellskitchenfleamarket.com

business credits

HANS BLOMQUIST
www.agentbauer.com
Endpapers; 1; 7–9; 10 right; 11; 12; 13; 14 below centre; 15 above; 15 below centre; 16–18; 20–21; 24 above and below left; 25; 28 right; 29; 31 below right 33; 36 above centre and above right; 40 left; 41; 44 below left; 47.

OLIVER GUSTAV
Nybrogade 16
1250 Copenhagen
Denmark
T: +45 27 37 46 30
E: mail@olivergustav.com
www.olivergustav.com
Pages 15 below right; 44 below right; 76–88.

JOSEPHINE RYAN
Antique dealer, decorator, stylist and writer
www.josephineryanantiques.co.uk
House available for rent at www.josephineryanfrance.co.uk
T: +44 (0)7973 336149
Pages 3–4; 34; 36 below left; 36 below centre; 50–63.

LA MAISON PUJOL B&B
Contact: Famille Mosser
17 rue Frédérick Mistral
11600 Conques sur Orbiel
France
T: +33 9 81 41 38 18
E: info@lamaisonpujol.net
www.lamaisonpujol.net
Pages 2; 5; 35 right; 39; 94–99.

MONIQUE MEIJ-BEEKMAN
Shop: Voorhaven 7
Voorhaven 7
2871 CH Schoonhaven
The Netherlands
E: info@voorhaven7.nl
www.voorhaven7.nl
Pages 10 left; 22–23; 38; 44 above; 130–141.

PASCALE PALUN
Vox Populi
17 rue Thiers
84000 Avignon
T: +33 4 90 85 70 25
E: vox.populi.deco@wanadoo .fr
www.voxpopulideco.com
Pages 19; 24 above right; 24 below right; 30 -31; 40 right; 42–43; 44 above right; 45; 142–153; 160.

REINI SMIT STYLIST
E: reini@quicknet.nl
Pages 112–121.

JACQUES BASTIDE
Architect: Jean Louis Tetrel
Pages 14 below left; 26–27; 37; 46; 100–111.

ALFONSO VALLÈS
www.alfonsovallès.fr
Pages 14 above right; 15 below left; 28 left; 32; 35 left; 36 below right; 64–75.

STELLA WILLING
www.bystella.com
www.barmoustache.nl
Pages 36 above left; 48–49; 122–129.

JEAN-MARC DIMANCHE
V.I.T.R.I.O.L. agency
www.vitriol-agency.com
and
XY architecture – Yes Bour & Xavier Esselinck
www.xyarchitecture.com
Pages 14 above left; 14 above centre; 14 below right; 86–93.

picture credits

Endpapers: From the author's home in Paris, www.agentbauer.com; 1 From the author's home in Paris, www.agentbauer.com; 2 La Maison Pujol (B&B) near Carcassonne, owned by Aurélie and René Mosser, www.lamaisonpujol.net; 3–4 Josephine Ryan – Antique Dealer/Decorator/Stylist/Writer www.josephineryanantiques.co.uk; 5 La Maison Pujol (B&B) near Carcassonne, owned by Aurélie and René Mosser, www.lamaisonpujol.net; 7–9 From the author's home in Paris, www.agentbauer.com; 10 left The home of artist and antiques dealer and interior designer Monique Meij-Beekman in the Netherlands; 10 right–13 From the author's home in Paris, www.agentbauer.com; 14 above left and centre "La villa des Ombelles" the family home of Jean-Marc Dimanche, Chairman of V.I.T.R.I.O.L. agency, www.vitriol-factory.com; 14 above right The home of Virginie Denny, fashion designer and Alfonso Vallès, painter; 14 below left The home of Jacques Bastide in Arles, France; 14 below centre From the author's home in Paris, www.agentbauer.com; 14 below right "La villa des Ombelles" the family home of Jean-Marc Dimanche, Chairman of V.I.T.R.I.O.L. agency, www.vitriol-factory.com; 15 above From the author's home in Paris, www.agentbauer.com; 15 below left The home of Virginie Denny, fashion designer and Alfonso Vallès, painter; 15 below centre From the author's home in Paris, www.agentbauer.com; 15 below right The home of antiques dealer and interior designer Oliver Gustav in Copenhagen; 16–18 From the author's home in Paris, www.agentbauer.com; 19 Vox Populi, the studio of the artist/designer Pascale Palun, in Avignon; 20–21 From the author's home in Paris, www.agentbauer.com; 22–23 The home of artist and antiques dealer and interior designer Monique Meij-Beekman in the Netherlands; 24 above and below left From the author's home in Paris, www.agentbauer.com; 24 above and below right Vox Populi, the studio of the artist/designer Pascale Palun, in Avignon; 25 From the author's home in Paris, www.agentbauer.com; 26–27 The home of Jacques Bastide in Arles, France; 28 left The home of Virginie Denny, fashion designer and Alfonso Vallès, painter; 28 right–29 From the author's home in Paris, www.agentbauer.com; 30–31 Vox Populi, the studio of the artist/designer Pascale Palun, in Avignon; 31 below right From the author's home in Paris, www.agentbauer.com; 32 The home of Virginie Denny, fashion designer and Alfonso Vallès, painter; 33 From the author's home in Paris, www.agentbauer.com; 34 Josephine Ryan – Antique Dealer/Decorator/Stylist/Writer www.josephineryanantiques.co.uk; 35 left The home of Virginie Denny, fashion designer and Alfonso

Vallès, painter; 35 right La Maison Pujol (B&B) near Carcassonne, owned by Aurélie and René Mosser, www.lamaisonpujol.net; 36 above left Stella Willing stylist/designer and owner of house in Amsterdam; 36 above centre and right From the author's home in Paris, www.agentbauer.com; 36 below left and centre Josephine Ryan – Antique Dealer/Decorator /Stylist/Writer www.josephineryanantiques.co.uk; 36 below right The home of Virginie Denny, fashion designer and Alfonso Vallès, painter; 37 The home of Jacques Bastide in Arles, France; 38 The home of artist and antiques dealer and interior designer Monique Meij-Beekman in the Netherlands; 39 La Maison Pujol (B&B) near Carcassonne, owned by Aurélie and René Mosser, www.lamaisonpujol.net; 40 left From the author's home in Paris, www.agentbauer.com; 40 right Vox Populi, the studio of the artist/designer Pascale Palun, in Avignon; 41 From the author's home in Paris, www.agentbauer.com; 42–43 Vox Populi, the studio of the artist/designer Pascale Palun, in Avignon; 44 above left The home of artist and antiques dealer and interior designer Monique Meij-Beekman in the Netherlands; 44 above right Vox Populi, the studio of the artist/designer Pascale Palun, in Avignon; 44 below left From the author's home in Paris, www.agentbauer.com; 44 below right The home of antiques dealer and interior designer Oliver Gustav in Copenhagen; 45 Vox Populi, the studio of the artist/designer Pascale Palun, in Avignon; 46 The home of Jacques Bastide in Arles, France; 47 From the author's home in Paris, www.agentbauer.com; 48–49 Stella Willing stylist/designer and owner of house in Amsterdam; 50–63 Josephine Ryan – Antique Dealer/Decorator/Stylist/Writer www.josephineryanantiques.co.uk; 64–75 The home of Virginie Denny, fashion designer and Alfonso Vallès, painter; 76–85 The home of antiques dealer and interior designer Oliver Gustav in Copenhagen; 86–93 "La villa des Ombelles" the family home of Jean-Marc Dimanche, Chairman of V.I.T.R.I.O.L. agency, www.vitriol-factory.com; 94–99 La Maison Pujol (B&B) near Carcassonne, owned by Aurélie and René Mosser, www.lamaisonpujol.net; 100–111 The home of Jacques Bastide in Arles, France; 112–121 The house of stylist Reini Smit in the Netherlands, reini@quicknet.nl; 122–129 Stella Willing stylist/designer and owner of house in Amsterdam; 130–141 The home of artist and antiques dealer and interior designer Monique Meij-Beekman in the Netherlands; 142–153 Vox Populi, the studio of the artist/designer Pascale Palun, in Avignon; 160 Vox Populi, the studio of the artist/designer Pascale Palun, in Avignon.

index

Figures in italics indicate captions.

acknowledgments

First of all, my greatest thank you to Debi for working on this book with me, for taking the most beautiful pictures, and for all the great moments of friendship we shared while shooting locations around Europe. Also a big thank you to Leslie, Annabel, Jess and Helen, and a special thank you to Megan for great team work on the layouts, making a beautiful and simple book. Thank you also to everyone else at Ryland Peters & Small for giving me the opportunity to do this book.

Thank you to all the home owners who opened their doors and let us take over their homes for a day, and for their kindness on the days we were shooting, serving us both coffee and lunch.

Frederick, Emil and Felix, thank you for coping with having an upside-down home while shooting pictures for the Natural Elements section, and spending hours in the car going to flea markets and antique fairs to find all the very special stuff I always seem to just need.

And, last but not least, a big thank you to my parents for letting me explore my own way from a very early age.